Contents

Did you know that the Wright Brothers invented and flew the first airplane in 1903 and today some airplanes are longer than the length of their actual first flight? Or did you know that airplanes are the safest way to travel and the risk of being killed in a plane crash is 1 in 11 million? Or have you ever wondered if it's really necessary to turn off electronic devices inside an airplane?

In this book, you will find the answers to these questions and much more!

The **Big Book of Aviation Facts** is an illustrated compilation of curiosities, statistics, military, history, technical and fun facts.

It contains over 100 incredible, interesting, entertaining and educational facts about the world of aviation among a nice selection of awesome photos.

Enjoy, be amazed and have fun, all while learning all you need to know about aviation!

Fun Facts & Curiosities

Savings

In 1987 American Airlines saved $40,000 by removing one olive from each salad served in first class.

Passengers pushing a plane?

While the outside of an aircraft can reach -60 degrees Fahrenheit when it's cruising at 35,000 feet, similar ground temperatures can stop a plane in its tracks. In 2014, when temperatures hit about -47 degrees Fahrenheit at Igarka Airport in Russia, a Tupelov-134 jet's landing gear braking system actually froze, leading passengers to do their best to help: they actually got out to try to push the 61,640-pound plane.

Pilots frequently fall asleep on the job

So, who's flying your plane, exactly? Maybe no one at least for portions of the flight. According to a 2017 report by the British Airline Pilots Association (BALPA), among a group of 500 pilots polled, 43 percent admitted to accidentally falling asleep while manning the plane, while 31 percent admitted to waking up from a nap to find their co-pilot sleeping, as well.

Why pilots and co-pilots eat different meals on a flight?

Pilots and co-pilots are advised not to eat the same meals when they are working. If something is wrong with the meal (like food poisoning), the other pilot will not be affected and can take over. The rule is not mandated by the Federal Aviation Administration, but most airlines have their own rules about it.

Why do I never see the pilots?

Pilots are 75% more likely to be at the front door saying goodbye to passengers after a good landing than after a bad landing.

President and Vice President of the United States never fly together

It's probably not surprising to learn that the President and Vice President of the United States never fly together nor do they fly with the Speaker of the House of Representatives. As the first, second, and third in the chain of succession, a craft carrying any two of these passengers could lead to serious disruption to the U.S. government if it crashed. For similar reasons, Prince Charles and his son, Prince William, don't fly together, as they are second and third in line to the throne.

How much air does a 767 airplane suck?

The Boeing 767 sucks in enough air through its engines to fill a Good Year Blimp in 7 seconds.

Windshield cost

One windshield or window frame of a Boeing 747-400's cockpit costs as much as a BMW car.

Is it really necessary to turn off electronic devices inside an airplane?

Few rules are more confounding to airline passengers than those regarding the use of cell phones and portable electronic devices. Passengers should know that the restrictions pertaining to computers, iPads, and certain other devices are not about electronic interference.

TURN OFF CELL PHONES

The main reason laptops need to be put away is to prevent them from becoming high-speed projectiles in the event of an impact or sudden deceleration. Cellular communication can 'potentially' interfere with cockpit equipment, but in all likelihood, it doesn't.
The machines and electronics in airplanes and cockpits have been designed to shield against any interference. The risks are minimal, or else phones would be collected or inspected visually rather than "relying on the honor system."

Where is safer to sit on a plane ?

Sitting in the tail of an airplane improves chances of accident survival. According to Popular Mechanics, sitting in the tail of an airplane improves chances of accident survival by 40%.

The world's most frequent flyer

The world's most frequent flier just racked up a record setting 21 million miles flown. That's nearly 844 times around the equator.

The 21-million-mile man: Tom Stuker is the world's most frequent flyer. "I'm a flying junkie," the 65-year-old Nutley, New Jersey resident told The Post. "If I spend more than a week in one place, I'm like, 'I gotta get back in the air.' I'm more afraid to be on the ground than in the air."
In July in 2019, he broke his own record of 20 million, which was set only in January.

Can you imagine a transparent plane?

Airbus is working on a transparent plane that would offer passengers a 360-degree view as they fly.

Excess weight of luggage. What do you think about this?

A man once wore 70 items of clothing in a Chinese airport to avoid a baggage charge.

Surgical operation on board

A surgeon performed an operation on a plane using a coat hanger sterilized with brandy after a passenger started complaining of chest pain.
Angus Wallace assessed the woman and determined that she was most likely suffering from tension pneumothorax. He used part of a coat hanger sterilized with brandy to insert a tube into her chest cavity.

Baby Tiger

A woman tried to smuggle a baby tiger onto an airplane by sedating it and then placing it in a suitcase with stuffed toy tigers. However, her plan was foiled when the X-ray in the security check showed that one of the "stuffed toys" actually had bones.

A plane with a detachable cabin?

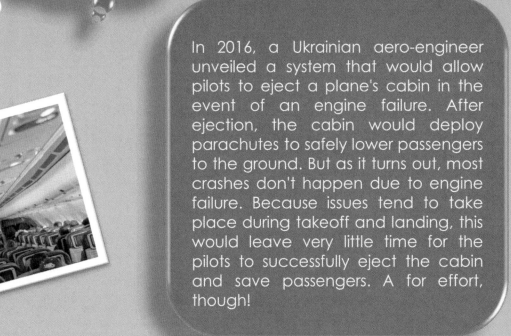

In 2016, a Ukrainian aero-engineer unveiled a system that would allow pilots to eject a plane's cabin in the event of an engine failure. After ejection, the cabin would deploy parachutes to safely lower passengers to the ground. But as it turns out, most crashes don't happen due to engine failure. Because issues tend to take place during takeoff and landing, this would leave very little time for the pilots to successfully eject the cabin and save passengers. A for effort, though!

Is it possible to open the door of the plane during the flight?

It is impossible to open a door during a flight. If a cabin is pressurized and an airplane door came open in midflight at a high altitude, the sudden opening could cause items and people to get sucked out. However, pressurization in the cabin and a plug-type door (a door that is bigger than the opening), makes it near impossible for even multiple people to open a door during a flight!

You are about 7% of the distance to space during flights

Sometimes, it can feel like you are astronomically high in the air when you're on a plane. However, you might be surprised to discover that you're actually only 7 percent of the distance it would take for you to get into space. Planes can fly much higher than their average altitude of 30,000, but they don't because doing so would present health risks to those insides.

Pointing a laser pointer at a plane is a serious crime

Drive your pets crazy with a laser pointer all you want, but never aim that annoying red dot at a plane. According to 18 U.S. Code Section 39A, if you point a laser pointer at a plane or its flight path, you can enjoy up to five years in prison to think about what you've done.

Contrails of a Plane

The contrails of a plane primarily consist of frozen, crystallized water vapor. They also contain carbon dioxide, nitrogen oxide, sulfate particles, and soot. Some conspiracy theorists claim that the government and military have planted harmful chemicals in contrails

Fear of flying?

The scientific name is aerophobia and is totally normal.
More than 80% of the population is afraid of flying. 5% completely abandons flights and take alternative forms of travel. Despite crashes being very rare, 6.5 percent of Americans suffer from aerophobia or a fear of flying.

The Anxiety and Depression Association of America says that most of this stress originates from the total loss of control or possibly the feeling of being trapped.

DON'T PANIC

Eating an entire plane?

Michel Lotito holds the world record for eating an entire aircraft, piece by piece. In the 1990s, he spent two years eating a Cessna 150. Lotito wasted nothing on his plate; he consumed everything from the upholstered leather seats and the tires.
He is actually famous for deliberately consuming indigestible objects. He came to be known as Monsieur Mangetout ("Mr. Eat-All")

Human Head

A woman flying into Florida tried to smuggle a human head (along with hair, teeth, and skin) from Haiti in order to keep away evil spirits. She was charged with smuggling a human head into the U.S. without proper documentation. She was also charged with failure to declare the head and for transporting hazardous material.
She told authorities she had obtained the package in Haiti for "use as a part of her voodoo beliefs,

Smuggling a dead relative

A woman and her daughter were arrested when they tried to smuggle the woman's dead husband in a wheelchair onto a plane.
The 91-year-old deceased man was pushed in a wheelchair through the airport wearing sunglasses before check-in staff became suspicious and he was prevented from boarding the plane.

65 Snakes!!

A woman from Stockholm, Sweden, attempted to smuggle 65 live baby snakes onto an airplane by placing them in her bra. She also had six lizards under her shorts.

HISTORY FACTS

Wright Brothers First Flight

The Wright brothers invented and flew the first airplane in 1903.
December 17, The Wright Brothers make four flights in their Flyer at Kitty Hawk, North Carolina following years of research and development. Orville Wright takes off first and flies 120 ft (37 m)in 12 seconds. On the fourth effort, which is considered by some to be the first true controlled, powered heavier than air flight, Wilbur flies 852 ft (260 m) in 59 seconds.

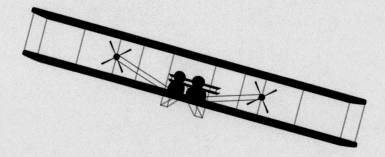

Orville Wright did not sit in the Wright Flyer during its first flight. Instead, he lay flat on the lower wing in the middle of the plane.
Neil Armstrong carried a piece of the Wright Flyer with him to the moon. Today, the Boeing 787 can fly 10,000 miles on a single tank of gas.

First Woman to solo fly

Raymonde de Laroche of France is the first woman to pilot a solo flight in an airplane in 1909. She did become the world's first licensed female pilot on March 8, 1910.

The first woman to fly solo across the Atlantic Ocean

Amelia Earhart (1897–1937) was the first woman to fly solo across the Atlantic Ocean. For her solo transatlantic crossing in 1932, she was awarded a Distinguished Flying Cross by the U.S. Congress.

She also helped create "The Ninety-Nines," which was an organization for female pilots, who also achieved many other notable accomplishments.

The first to fly solo nonstop across the Atlantic Ocean

Charles Lindbergh was the first to fly solo nonstop across the Atlantic Ocean from, New York to Paris, on May 20–21, 1927. The trip covered 3,631 miles and took 33 hours 29 minutes. Charles Lindbergh is arguably the most famous pilot in history. Nicknamed "Slim," "Lucky Lindy," and "The Lone Eagle" he was an author, inventor, military officer, explorer, and social activist.

Around the world without landing

In 1986, a plane called Voyager flew all the way around the world without landing or refueling.

The sound barrier was broken in 1947

Pilot Chuck Yeager astonished the world with his record, breaking flying skills. This U.S. Air Force vet learned to fly as a fighter pilot during World War II. Using the Bell X-1 rocket jet, he flew faster than the speed of sound: 662 miles per hour at 40,000 feet.

Breaking the sound barrier at 89 years old

Chuck Yeager, the first man to fly faster than the speed of sound, revived his feat on October 14, 2012, in an F-15 Eagle, to celebrate the 65th anniversary of breaking the sound barrier. He was 89 years old.

15

The fastest commercial plane flew at twice the speed of sound

The Concorde, which offered flights continuously from 1976 to 2003, traveled at twice the speed of sound. The supersonic jet could achieve speeds up to 1,354 miles per hour.

The world's oldest airline

Dutch airline **KLM** has the longest continuously operating record in the world. The Dutch company was founded in 1919 and first took flight in May of 1920. Its inaugural flight was from the Netherlands to Croydon Airport in London.

Safety record

Qantas is the world's second-oldest airline, established in 1920, and also has the best safety record with no fatal crashes in their history.

Deadliest Accident in Aviation History

In 1977, the deadliest crash in the history of aviation happened on the ground. Pan Am Flight 1736 and KLM Flight 4805, both Boeing 747s, crashed into one another in Tenerife, Spain. However, as CBS News reports, it wasn't an error on either pilot's part, per se—low fog made visibility poor, and the airport's runways were overly congested, leading to the two planes colliding, killing 583 passengers and crew members in the resulting fire.

Air travel is the second safest form of transportation. Only the elevator/escalator is safer, although it would take quite some time to travel 1,000 miles on an escalator.

Check-in

The internet and online check-in were first introduced by Alaska Airlines in 1999.

First class 1970

British Airways reputedly invented the cabin between economy and first in the late 1970s, with the name "Club Class", but the name "Business Class" actually originated with Qantas in 1979.

F4 Phantom II

The McDonnell Douglas F-4 Phantom II is a tandem two-seat, twin-engine, all-weather, long-range supersonic jet interceptor and fighter-bomber originally developed for the United States Navy.
It was called "World's Leading Distributor of MiG Parts" because it destroyed so many MiG fighters (MiG is a supersonic jet fighter and interceptor aircraft, designed in the Soviet Union).

Make sure the plane is truly damaged before being ejected

In 1989, a Soviet pilot ejected a perfectly working MIG 23 thinking the plane's engine had failed. The MiG flew over 560 miles, crossing Germany before running out of fuel and crashing into a house in Belgium killing one teenager.

Who got the best souvenir?

During WW2, Russian Fighter pilot S. Kuzniecov flew himself home by stealing the Nazi fighter plane that shot him down. The German pilot landed at a nearby flat strip of land to collect souvenirs from his prey and to kill the Soviet pilot if he was still alive. he never saw it coming!
But Kuzniecov's troubles didn't end there! Soviet pilots didn't take kindly to German planes approaching their airbases. The Russian managed to survive getting shot down by the Nazis and almost died trying to avoid getting shot down by his comrades!

Leave your enemy with no spare parts

Every last F14 Tomcat is being shredded to prevent spares reaching Iran, who are still flying the ones sold to them by the US in the '70s.

Single wing landing

In 1983, an Israeli pilot successfully landed an F-15 with only one wing. In fact, he didn't realize the extent of the damage until after landing and stated he would have ejected had he known.

Air Force One

In June 1974, while President Nixon was on his way to a scheduled stop in Syria, Syrian fighter jets intercepted Air Force One to act as escorts. However, the Air Force One crew was not informed in advance and, as a result, took evasive action including a dive.

Start a rumor to hide top secret technology

During WW2, the British government started a rumor that excessive carrot consumption gave gunners night vision. They did this so as not to alert Germans of Royal Air Force's new radar technology after they shot down German aircraft on night raids ... and the Germans believed it! Germans fighters then started eating large quantities of carrots.

Go fast!

The Lockheed SR-71 Blackbird strategic reconnaissance aircraft was so fast, the designers did not even consider evasive maneuvers; the pilot was simply instructed to accelerate and out-fly any threat, including missiles.

Even better

As impressive as Lockheed SR-71 was, it had a secret older brother (the A-12) which was even faster, lighter, and had a higher service ceiling.

Invincible in the air

The F-15 Eagle in all Air Forces has a combined air-to-air combat record of 104 kills to 0 losses. No air superiority versions of the F-15 (A/B/C/D models) have been shot down by enemy forces.

INSIDE DE CABIN

Jetlag

The best ways to beat jetlag are to reset your internal clock. Here a few tips:

a. Try to shift your sleep pattern: go to bed one hour earlier or later depending on which direction you are flying.

b. If you're going on a really long flight (for instance, from Australia to Europe) take melatonin pills for 2-3 days before the trip.

c. Drink ginger tea.

d. When on the plane, go to sleep as soon as possible, don't take sleeping pills on board, and avoid alcohol and also coffee.

e. When you arrive, stay up until its bedtime wherever you are. Walk around in the sun, and if you must nap, keep it under an hour.

Turbulence is the top cause of nonfatal plane injuries.

Aircraft radar cannot detect turbulence. Turbulence can occur in clear, cloudless weather as well as in bad weather. It is the number one cause of in-flight injuries. Turbulence is caused by several factors, including jet streams and masses of rising hot air. Other causes include currents from storms, other planes, or air passing over mountains. Worryingly incidents of severe turbulence are on the rise, caused by the increase in carbon dioxide in the atmosphere, it is yet another negative effect of climate change.

Your taste buds change in flight.

Good news for those who don't find airplane meals particularly palatable: you're not actually tasting as much of them as you might imagine. According to the folks at JetBlue, the difference in air pressure and the low humidity in a plane's cabin make it more difficult for your taste buds to register sweet and salty flavors, for example, our ability to perceive salty tastes is weakened, so tomato juice tastes sweet.

Airplane blankets aren't always washed between passengers

If you're thinking of cozying up under one of those airplane blankets, think again. According to one report published in the Wall Street Journal, some airlines clean their blankets as infrequently as once every 30 days.

Water please!!

Cabin air is drier than most deserts. At under 20 percent humidity, the typical cabin is exceptionally dry and dehydrating due to cruising at high altitudes. Humidifying a cabin is too costly and could cause corrosion.
According to one estimate, you can lose about two cups of water from your body for every hour you spend flying. Drink water before, during, and after a long flight

The dirtiest place on the plane isn't the bathroom.

As it so happens, the filthiest place on a plane is that tray table you're eating your meal off of!!
According to a study conducted by TravelMate, tray tables hosted 2,155 colony-forming bacterial units (CFU) per square inch. In comparison, the button to flush the toilet had just 265 CFU in the same amount of space.

Clean air

The air on airplanes is filtered by the same technology that filters the air in hospitals, so while the tray table may harbor germs, the air is clean.

Airplane bathrooms can be opened from the outside

While flipping that latch inside the bathroom that turns the door sign to "occupied" may give you some semblance of privacy, there's an easy way for flight personnel to get in if they need to. Underneath that lavatory sign, there's a switch that allows the flight crew to open the door if they're concerned about your safety or the safety of other passengers.

Long haul flights have secret bedrooms and a bathroom for flight attendants.

If flight attendants work on long haul flights which can last upwards of 12 hours they need time to properly rest. So, airlines have installed secret sleeping quarters above the main cabin with seven or eight beds, and occasionally a separate bathroom as well. They can also enjoy in-flight entertainment while inside these secret chambers. That must be how they keep up their cheery demeanor on those long flights.

The best-dressed flight attendants

Thai Airways cabin crew are required to wear separate uniforms on land and in the air. They change into traditional Thai dresses in the air, while on the ground they wear a corporate purple suit. Any crew of a nationality other than Thai are not allowed to wear the dress. So glamorous is the Thai Airways uniform that it made it on to our Style In The Aisles, The Top Ten Cabin Crew Uniforms 2015.

Flight attendants per passengers

The specific rules regarding flight attendants vary among airlines and between countries. But in the UK and US, there must be at least one FA per 50 passengers.

STATISTICS

The world's busiest commercial airport

The busiest commercial airport in the world is the Hartsfield- Jackson Airport (ATL) in Atlanta, with more than 970.000 airplane movements a year.

The world's largest passenger plane

The world's largest passenger plane is the Airbus A380. It is a double-decker four-engine jetliner. It made its first flight on April 27, 2005.

The Airbus A380 has about 4 million parts produced by 1,500 companies from 30 countries around the world.

The wing-span of the A380 is longer than the aircraft itself. The wingspan is 262.5ft (80m), the length is 238.5ft (72.7m) and is longer than the Wright Brothers' first flight of 120ft (36.5m).

World's smallest plane

The Bede BD-5 microjet weighs only 358.8 pounds and has a wingspan of only 14.5 feet. Though minuscule, this jet can reach speeds of over 300 miles per hour, which is a little under half of the speed of sound.

World's largest plane

The Antonov AN-225 cargo jet is the largest plane in the world, has an impressive maximum takeoff weight of 591.7 tons It is nearly as big as a football field from nose to tail and wingtip to wingtip. It was originally built to transport a spaceplane.

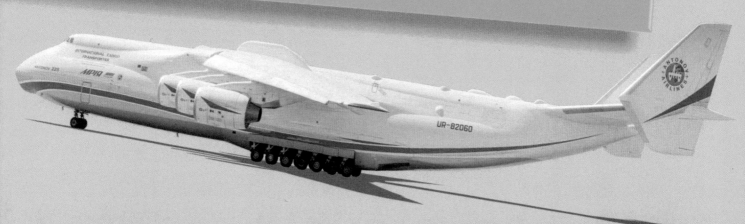

The longest military plane is six stories long

The U.S. military's gargantuan C-5 has a wingspan is 222.8 feet, with each wing measuring the length of a basketball court. At six stories tall, it can also carry more than 250 million pounds and 350 passengers, even with equipment on board. It is so big that many Air Force bases have had to cut large holes in hangar doors to keep it indoors. Its length of 143 feet is longer than the Wright Brother's first flight of 120 feet.

Only 5% of the world's population has ever been on an airplane

Though the aviation sector is growing rapidly, according to the statistics only 5% of the world's population has ever flown on an airplane. Many people, especially from underdeveloped regions, have never ever been in an aircraft and it is not likely that they will have an opportunity to fly in all of their lives. However, at the same time, a small minority of the world's population fly very regularly.

Largest Airlines by fleet size

American Airlines (including US Airways) is the largest by fleet size with 935 aircraft in 2019.

Thanksgiving is the busiest time of year for air travel in the USA.

With Thanksgiving being an American holiday rather than one with religious roots, it's a time of year when millions of people are trying to fly somewhere to be with (or away from) their loved ones. It's estimated that over 30 million people travel during that week. Though it has been widely reported that Thanksgiving Eve is the busiest travel day, it's actually the Sunday after when everyone is trying to get back to wherever they originally traveled from.

Most Expensive Flights In The World

Etihad Airways Residence, New York-Abu Dhabi for $64,000. "The Residence" has been dubbed a three-room "penthouse in the sky" by the luxury Gulf carrier. The price of your ticket includes a 125 sqft cabin as well as limousine transfers. The Residence strives to offer the same luxuries as a five-star hotel. Passengers enjoy the services of a private VIP travel concierge, who organize everything about your private check-in, arrival, limousine transfers, and more.

Risk of being killed in a plane crash

The risk of being killed in a plane crash is 1 in 11 million. The odds improve significantly if you're nice to your crew. Air travel is the second safest form of transportation. Only the elevator/escalator is safer, although it would take quite some time to travel 1,000 miles on an escalator.

Longest commercial Flight

Due to the 2019–20 coronavirus pandemic and the impossibility of transit in the USA through Los Angeles International Airport, Air Tahiti Nui set up in March 2020, a few direct flights between Papeete and Paris,

How many people and planes are there in the sky?

While you may only see the occasional plane pass by overhead, that doesn't mean the sky isn't full of them. In fact, according to the FAA, there are 5,000 planes in the air over the United States at any moment in time, and more than 8,000 flying across the globe.

At any given moment, there are about 61,000 people airborne over the mainland United States & over two million passengers board over 30,000 flights each day.

Usual commercial airplane speed.

Airplanes usually fly at a cruising speed of 575 mph (925 kmh). Jets have flown much faster and even broken the sound barrier, but most commercial flights stick to speed in this range optimizing their costs.

Technical Facts

Black boxes aren't actually black

The black box, also known as the Flight Data Recorder, is actually painted bright orange. The heat resistant paint used to coat the boxes' exteriors comes in a highlighter orange hue, which also happens to make them easier to find in case of an accident.

Some planes can fly for more than five hours after one of their engines goes out

ETOPS or extended twin operations is a designation that indicates the length of time a twin-engine plane can safely cruise to with one inoperative engine. In 2014, the Boeing 787 Dreamliner earned 330 minute ETOPS certifications, meaning it can stay safely operational on just one engine for more than five hours before needing to land.

Oxygen masks aren't intended to last the whole flight

According to a report from the Air Accident Investigation & Aviation Safety Board, those masks only provide 12 to 15 minutes of continuous airflow on a 737. Luckily, that's typically just the amount of time needed for your flight to find a safe landing spot.

Airplanes can trigger lightning

When a plane passes through clouds, the static created can actually spur the development of lightning. Fortunately, even if your plane is struck, you're likely pretty safe. There hasn't been a lightning-related plane crash in the United States since 1967, and increasing safety measures have made lightning strikes less dangerous to passengers than ever before.

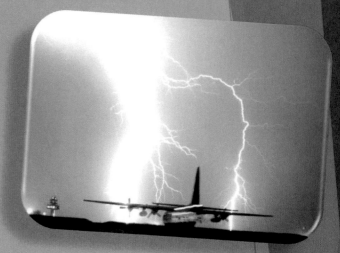

Dimming the aircraft's lights serves a purpose beyond sleep

While it's nice to imagine that airlines are simply hoping you'll get in some restful sleep, that's not exactly the truth. In fact, dimming the lights aboard a plane helps passengers' eyes adjust to the dark, an essential component in helping them survive should there be a sudden nighttime evacuation.

Pilots who fly internationally must know English

English is the international language of flight. All flight controllers and all commercial pilots who fly on international flights are required to speak English.

Takeoff and landing are the most dangerous times during a flight

According to a report from Boeing, 13 percent of fatal accidents occur during a flight's takeoff and initial climb, or the first three minutes of a flight. However, the descent and landing, or the final eight minutes of the flight, are far deadlier, accounting for 48 percent of all fatal accidents.

The average age of a commercial aircraft

The lifespan of an airliner is not truly measured in time. Instead, it is counted based on pressurization cycles. Each time an aircraft is pressurized during a flight its fuselage is subjected to stress. The "lifespan" of an aircraft is reached when there are certain metal fatigues and cracks which may pose danger. The "service life of 20 years" is generally expressed by approximate figures of 51,000 flight hours and 75,000 pressurization cycles for most aircraft. If an aircraft is used on long haul routes it experiences relatively few pressurization cycles in its "life" and can remain airworthy far beyond 20 years.

Mayday

Mayday' is derived from the French word m'aidez, which means help me!

A Boeing 747 tank can hold 48,445 gallons of fuel

That's 17,248 times the amount of fuel held in the gas tank of a Dodge Ram pickup truck. However, not all of that fuel is being used during a single flight, in fact, the plane only uses an average of five gallons of fuel per mile, meaning a 3,450 mile trip from New York to London only requires about a third of the plane's total fuel capacity.

Descend

Nearly every plane glides during its descent. It is common for planes to descend at what pilots call "flight idle" with the engines still operating and powering, but providing no push. If the engines quit outright, the glide itself would be no different. From 30,000 feet, pilots can plan on a hundred miles' worth of glide.

Passenger and luggage weight

Passengers and their luggage only account for 10 percent of a plane's total weight. Fuel is the biggest factor, sometimes accounting for a third or more of a plane's total heft.

Fuel efficient

70% of aircraft in service today are over 70% more fuel efficient per seat kilometer than the first jets in the 1960s.

A Boeing 747 is made up of six million parts

Boeing 747 is the most well known wide body commercial airliner and cargo transportation aircraft frequently referred to as the Queen of the Skies or the Jumbo Jet. A Boeing 747 is made up of six million parts which are made to be all controlled by a few pilots sitting up front with switches and buttons under their fingertips.

Airplane tires are inflated to about six times the PSI of car tires

The real reason airplane tires rarely pop, even though they're carrying a huge amount of weight? It's not their just thickness that contributes to their strength under pressure. According to a Wired report, airplane tires are pumped to roughly 200 psi about six times the psi of an average car tire. In fact, according to an experiment recorded by National Geographic, a Boeing 737's tires can withstand over 900 psi before bursting.

Autopilot

Autopilot is usually turned on during most of an airplane flight. The computer can make more precise adjustments, which leads to better fuel efficiency (except during turbulence). Autopilot is not typically used during takeoff or landing, although it is available to use.

Airport control tower windows

Aircraft control towers need to have constant visibility of the airfield at all times. To that end, the glass in tower windows is angled precisely at 15°, which prevents glare and reflections from blocking a controller's view of the runways.

How to differentiate an Airbus from a Boeing

The strobe lights on the wingtips of an Airbus make a double flash, on a Boeing they make a single flash.

There are 140 miles of wiring inside a Boeing 747

According to a report from technology company Tyco Electronics, which manufactures wire connectors for the aviation industry, a 747 can pack 750,000 feet, or 140 miles of wire inside it, weighing approximately 3,500 pounds in total.

Each engine on a Boeing 747 weighs almost 9,500 pounds

Another interesting fact about a Boeing 747 concerns its engine weight, which weighs almost 9,500 pounds (4,300 kg) and costs about 8 million USD.

The pilot may decide to dump fuel from its wings

If a plane needs to make an emergency landing, a pilot may decide to dump fuel from its wings. While it's not very common, it is a safety procedure to keep the plane from experiencing an overweight landing. The fuel usually evaporates before it reaches the ground.

Evacuated in 90 seconds

The FAA requires that all airplanes be capable of being evacuated in 90 seconds. It takes only a minute and a half for a fire to spread and engulf a plane.

747 family

The world-wide 747 fleets have logged more than 78 billion kilometers, equivalent to 101,500 trips to the moon and back. The 747 family has flown more than 5.6 billion people equivalent to 80% of the world's population.

The speed of a Boeing 747

Boeing 747 is not only one of the world's most recognizable aircraft, and the first wide-body ever produced. Another fascinating fact about this aircraft is that the maximum speed of a Boeing 747 is 594 Mi/h (955 km/h)

Boeing 747 fuel efficient

Boeing 747 is more fuel efficient than your car. The Boeing 747 burns approximately 1 gallon of fuel per second, or 5 gallons per mile. Reversing this gives us the figure of 0.2 gallons of fuel used per mile. This is much lower than the car's average fuel efficiency at about 25 miles per gallon. But, considering that it can carry about 500 people, you're actually getting 100 miles per gallon per person.

Made in the USA
Las Vegas, NV
16 November 2023

80799641R00024